SUPERBASE 12

EDWARDS

SUPERBASE 12

EDWARDS

Home of the Right Stuff

George Hall

Published in 1990 by Osprey Publishing
Limited
59 Grosvenor Street, London W1X 9DA

British Library Cataloguing in Publication
Data

Hall, George, *1941–*
   Edwards
   1. United States. Air Force. Military
aircraft. Illustrations
   I. Title   II. Series
   623.74′6′0973

ISBN 0 85045 928 1

Editor Tony Holmes
Designed by Stewart Cocking
Printed in Hong Kong

Front cover The test pilot carefully
manoeuvres his F-16A beneath the
towering tail of a KC-135 Stratotanker
high over the Edwards range.
Carrying full Air Force Systems
Command markings on the tail, this
Fighting Falcon is just one of 17
assigned to 6512nd Test Squadron

Back cover Cruising along at height
over Edwards, a veteran RF-4C
Phantom II clearly stands out against
the sky blue background. The glossy
paint job is a trademark of Test
Squadron Phantom IIs

Title pages An impressive view of
the long ramp at Edwards. Besides
the solitary F-111A, 14 F-4 Phantom IIs
of various marks can be seen basking
in the hot California sunshine. Both of
these types are assigned to the
6512nd Test Squadron (TS), part of
the Air Force Systems Command
based at Edwards. The twin towers
which dominate the flightline are a
striking feature of the base

Right The nature of the flying at
Edwards necessitates that the rescue
facilities assigned to the base be
second to none, which is, of course,
the case. With the vast hard-baked
desert runways providing an
awesome backdrop, a solitary Air
Rescue Bell HH-1H Huey 'wock
wocks' its way across the base

Introduction

Located in the sizzling Mojave Desert 100 miles north of Los Angeles, Edwards Air Force Base is the home of the Air Force Flight Test Center, the premier aerospace test and research facility in the West. No active strategic or tactical units operate out of Edwards; all aircraft at the huge base are either in a flight test programme or in support of one. Practically every aircraft in the Air Force inventory over the past half-century was tested and evaluated by the Air Force Flight Test Center, a unit of the Air Force Systems Command.

The first residents of this desolate area, ranchers by the name of Corum, homesteaded the valley early in this century. When they established a village and requested a post office, officials disallowed the name 'Corum', as another town by that name already existed. So they reversed the spelling and came up with 'Muroc', a name that stuck through World War 2 and beyond. Muroc Army Air Field was the sight of many historic firsts, including the testing of America's first jet, the Bell XP-59 Airacomet, in 1942, and the flight of the X-1 beyond Mach 1 with then-Air Force Captain Chuck Yeager at the stick. This milestone was passed over Muroc Dry Lake on 14 October 1947.

The base was renamed Edwards AFB in 1950, after Captain Glen Edwards, an accomplished test pilot who had been killed in the crash of a YB-49 'Flying Wing' in 1948. No one can fail to notice the amazing resemblance between that ill-fated aircraft and the cosmic B-2 'Stealth Bomber'.

The Air Force Test Pilot School is a key Edwards tenant. Top Air Force pilots vie to be included in the one-year programme; they fly training hops in school A-7s, T-38s, F-4s, A-37s, and any other military aircraft from whatever branch they can manage to borrow for check rides. The school jets, plus most of the other test birds at Edwards, are among the few Air Force aircraft painted shiny white.

We'll get a look at a number of hot new jets in various stages of their test regimes. There's the F-15E dual-role Eagle, the long-range strike variant of the single-seat interceptor. The AFTI F-16 sports computer-controlled canards and exaggerated control surfaces that make the little Falcon even more of an eye-watering turner and burner. A quartet of B-1B bombers stays on at Edwards for continued testing of the exotic and troublesome computer software, the EC-130 *Combat Talon II*, complete with the fork-tongued Fulton Recovery System, skulks about the ranges on low-level missions. And of course the enormous 16,000 foot lakebed runway welcomes the returning space shuttle on its renewed flight schedule. Recently a B-1B streaked all the way from Texas to make a shuttle-style, 300-mph lakebed landing with its variable-geometry wings stuck dangerously in the far-aft, speed-of-heat position!

The folks at Edwards are enormously proud of their contribution to aerospace history, and they were enthusiastic about telling their story in the Osprey SUPERBASE series. We can't thank all the units and pilots who helped out with information, anecdotes and photo fly-bys individually; as the saying goes: 'You know who you are.' The base public affairs folks, in the persons of Lt Mike Rein, Lt Col Jerry Guess, and long-time Edwards expert Don Haley, were exceptionally helpful on this project. Special thanks also to Maj Lance Grace of the F-15E test programme and Capt Robert 'Tanker Bob' Mattes for some memorable photo opportunities.

Photo dope: As always, cameras are Nikon F-3s and F-4s, with a selection of Nikkor lenses ranging from 15 mm to 500 mm. Film was Kodachrome 64 exclusively. Most of the air-to-air photos were shot from a KC-135 tanker.

Contents

Right Where it all started, at least as far as American jet fighter history is concerned! Mounted sturdily on a plinth in the grounds of the base is this immaculate Bell P-59B Airacomet, airframe 422633 being one of 30 'B' models built for the US Army Air Force. A conservative design of which only 66 were eventually built by Bell, the Airacomet nevertheless gave both pilots and groundcrews a taste of things to come. The original XP-59A took to the skies for the first time on 1 October 1942

Veteran tester

The unmistakable shape of the pugnacious F-4 Phantom II, a shape which has darkened the flightline at Edwards for over 30 years. The base's association with the 'bent-winged wonder' began on 23 June 1958 when the original prototype Phantom II was ferried from McDonnell's plant at St Louis to California by the company's chief test pilot, Robert C Little. Although not quite of that vintage, this particular F-4D is no spring chicken, being built in 1966. While the line sergeant performs a quick visual of the front office, a compatriot toils away beneath the starboard wing changing a tyre

Above Proudly wearing the unique Air Force Systems Command (AFSC) emblem on the fin, this extremely clean RF-4C is just one of several recce F-4s assigned to the Air Force Flight Test Center (AFFTC)

Right Showing off its semi 'Coke bottle' fuselage to perfection, an F-4E belonging to the 6512nd TS nudges towards the author's camera ship, a KC-135. The high visibility paint scheme worn on all AFFTC F-4s has not changed significantly since the early 1960s when the Flight first acquired the venerable type

The F-4 fleet at Edwards has flown all manner of testing tasks over the past three decades, starting out as the new type under evaluation in the early sixties. Eventually things have turned full circle and the once 'new boy on the block' now performs the roll of high speed chase aircraft, amongst many others, for its frontline replacements

Preceding pages With the F-4 rapidly disappearing from frontline USAF service, a sight like this will soon be but a memory for both Phantom II drivers and enthusiasts alike. The AFFTC however, will continue to ply the skies above the rugged terrain which surrounds Edwards for a few years yet

Inset, preceding page Pitch out! The recce Phantom II pilot performs a text-book break and curves away from his formation leader who will soon be following him in his F-4E

Inset All the aircraft operated by the AFFTC are maintained in immaculate condition, the result of many hours spent toiling in the extremely hot sun by the flight's groundcrew. Sparkling against the deep blue sky, this immaculate F-4E belies its 20 years old vintage, a tribute to the elbow grease expended by the men and women back at base

Right A veteran F-4C heads up two slightly younger stablemates on the Edwards ramp. The 6512nd seem to be experiencing problems in deciding what colour to paint the radomes on their Phantom IIs! The original Air Force Phantom II, the F-4C, was equipped with a Westinghouse APQ-100 radar housed within the radome, and a small infrared seeker fairing beneath the aircraft's nose, although no seeker was ever fitted. The F-4E, as the penultimate Air Force Phantom II, was fitted with a Westinghouse AN/APQ-120 radar, and a General Electric M61-A1 20 mm Vulcan cannon beneath the radome

Above The 'ordies' complete the final securing checks on one of three 500 lb iron bombs attached to a triple ejector rack mounted to the inboard port wing pylon. This F-4E has had the cannon muzzle beneath the nose faired over. Behind the aircraft an OH-6 Loach, an AH-64 Apache, a T-33 Shooting Star and a P-51 Mustang share space on the ramp. The scoops either side of the F-4's radome channel air into the aircraft's air-conditioning unit

Left A selection of high visibility tails on the Edwards ramp. All of these F-4Es are from the same production batch and wear the Air Force Systems Command crest and the sharks teeth striping on their tailplanes

The AFFTC owns a pair of F-4s that are the oldest Phantom IIs in service anywhere. Along with production-line brother 63-7407, this F-4C, bearing the serial number 63-7408, left the St Louis factory in early 1963. This particular aircraft was the third F-4 accepted by the USAF for service, and one of 583 Charlie model Phantom IIs built

'Can you buy one of these in blue?' During the annual open house the venerable
F-4 is still a major drawcard with the thousands of visitors that swarm all over
the Edwards flightline

Eagle alternatives

Arguably the world's greatest air superiority fighter, the F-15 Eagle is now vying for the title of the most capable strike aircraft in service with any force across the globe. Much of the development work undertaken by the aircraft's manufacturer, McDonnell Douglas, and USAF's operational evaluations, have been combined into a single programme of exhaustive tests undertaken by the crews of the 6512nd TS. Wearing full squadron markings, one of several F-15Es assigned to the unit cruises high over the rugged Californian landscape

Externally the Strike Eagle looks
identical to its twin seat stablemate,
the F-15B/D. However, the engineers
at McDonnell Douglas have certainly
made changes to the aircraft
internally, the F-15E combining
vastly upgraded avionics and
pin-point weapons delivery with a
significantly strengthened fuselage
structure. Emblazoned with the AFSC
crest, the bulging conformal fuel
tanks add a little bit more 'waist' to
the normally slender proportions of
the Eagle

Showing the effects of the aircraft's incredible manoeuvrability, the pilot gently pulls the F-15E away from the author's camera. Besides its remarkable weapons delivery capabilities, the most astounding feature of the Strike Eagle is its ability to pull up to 9G throughout its entire flight envelope, even when fully armed and weighing in at a breathtaking 81,000 lb. Sixty per cent of the F-15E's fuselage structure has been restressed and strengthened for a service life of 16,000 hours, a figure which is double that of the earlier Eagle interceptors

Safely plugged in, the pilot and weapons systems officer watch the KC-135 intently as their mount is replenished. The internal fuel capacity of the Strike Eagle has been slightly reduced, from 2070 to 2019 US gallons, enabling McDonnell Douglas designers to install the more advanced avionics systems associated with this aircraft. With a full load of fuel, both internally and in the conformal tanks, the F-15E has an endurance of over five hours

Left Fuelled up and ready to continue on with the mission at hand, the pilot drifts back from the tanker. All the crews chosen to participate in the Strike Eagle Operational Test and Evaluation (OT&E) were hand-picked ex- F-15 fighter drivers, teamed up with veteran F-111 and F-4 back-seaters tasked with evaluating the navigation and weapons targeting capabilities of the F-15E

Above Carrying a load more likely to be seen on an F-15C, the Strike Eagle performs a knife edge turn. The many ordnance racks mounted onto both the conformal tanks and the fuselage can be seen, as well as the large metallic engine bay covers which differ slightly from those fitted to earlier F-15s. These covers are now made of SPF/DB (superplastic formed and diffusion bonded) titanium. This high-tech material allows McDonnell Douglas to manufacture the covers as one large piece, instead of many smaller ones, because of its incredible shaping qualities

Flying at an altitude seldom used by the crews of the 6512nd TS, a brace of Strike Eagles cruise over the inhospitable terrain which forms such a large part of the Edwards testing range. A total of 392 F-15Es are due to be procured by the USAF, McDonnell Douglas delivering five to six aircraft each month during the course of 1990. Currently transitioning onto the F-15E is the 4th Tactical Fighter Wing (TFW), based at Seymour-Johnson Air Force Base in North Carolina. Three units comprise the 4th TFW, with the 336th Tactical Fighter Squadron (TFS) being the first to trade in their venerable F-4Es for the new Strike Eagle. Eventually the wing will have 72 aircraft on strength, split evenly between the 334th, 335th and 336th Fighter Squadrons

Carrying a mix of Mk 82 500 lb and Mk 84 2000 lb bombs on the wing and fuselage hardpoints, and terrain following and targeting pods immediately beneath the intakes, an F-15E undergoes final preparation before the mission. An integral part of the aircraft's overall effectiveness, the LANTIRN (Low Altitude Navigation and Targeting Infra-red for Night) pod being carefully fitted to the hardpoint by the groundcrewman is the navigation part of the twin pod system. It contains a day/night automatic terrain-following radar and a night FLIR (Forward Looking Infra-red Radar), which gives the pilot an excellent picture of the terrain approaching him on his HUD (Head-up Display). Mounted below the LANTIRN pod is the Texas Instruments terrain-following radar, an ultra sensitive device which combines with the aircraft's internally mounted Hughes APG-70 radar to give the Strike Eagle an unparalleled low-level attack capability. The LANTIRN targeting pod is mounted beneath the port intake and gives the aircraft a day/night and bad-weather stand-off targeting capability using a high-resolution FLIR, a missile boresight correlator and a laser designator. The boresight correlator and the laser designator are used to deliver 'smart' weapons that the F-15E can carry, like the AGM-65 Maverick air-to-surface missile, or laser guided bombs

The dual role of the Strike Eagle is perfectly illustrated by the fully bombed up
F-15E positioned on the Edwards ramp during the base open house. The snug fit
of the stores pylon through the conformal tank is clearly evident in this view

Above right Devoid of all squadron markings and carrying an SUU-20/A practice bomb dispenser beneath the wing, an F-15E taxies out towards the last-check station before departure. The safety pin flags will be removed from the bombs after the groundcrew have checked that the dispenser is mounted correctly. The LANTIRN targeting pod can also be seen beneath the gaping intake

Below right Fully bombed up, an F-15E basks in the early morning sun. Virtually all of the F-15E's navigation/attack and electronic warfare systems have been successfully tested at Edwards since 1982 to allow the production Strike Eagle to be operationally capable right from the word go

Inset, overleaf Low visibility markings will be the norm on all Tactical Air Command F-15Es, a sinister scheme befitting the role of the aircraft

Preceding pages As clean as they come. The F-15 has been a part of the Edwards scene for many years, much of the evolutionary testing of the aircraft having taken place there. This 6512nd TS machine was one of the last F-15As built by McDonnell Douglas in 1977, and is being flown by Squadron Leader Rick Pope, on exchange from the Royal Australian Air Force

Right Adding 'talons' to the Eagle, groundcrewmen from the 6512nd position the last of four AIM-7F Sparrow missiles into the recessed fuselage mountings. The coloured safety tags which adorn the aircraft before flight have still to be removed, and the lower stability fins for the recently positioned Sparrow rounds to be added. This particular Eagle is a Delta model, one of several two-seaters in the squadron

The Raytheon AIM-7F Sparrow has been the principal armament of the F-15 since the aircraft first entered service back in 1974. A weapon that has been severely criticized over the years, the Sparrow saw extensive service in Vietnam and has been progressively developed to its present stage of sophistication, with the bitter lessons of the South-east Asian conflict clearly in mind. The successful maturity of the Sparrow is still open to conjecture, however, in light of the skirmish between Libyan MiG-23s and US Navy F-14s of VF-32 'Swordsmen' in January 1989. The Tomcat crews shot off two AIM-7Fs at the closing MiGs without registering any hits before finally bagging one with a third Sparrow and the other with an AIM-9L Sidewinder

'Gently does it.' The AIM-7F version of the Sparrow has solid-state electronics linked to a semi-active radar guidance system. The missile is effective against targets manoeuvring at up to 7G, and has a range of approximately 15 miles The Sparrow's replacement, the Hughes AIM-120A Advanced Medium Range Air-to-Air Missile (AMRAAM), is currently entering service with the 33rd Tactical Fighter Wing, equipped with the F-15C, based at Eglin Air Force Base in Florida

The Falcon family

To complete the stable of frontline fighter types operated by the 6512nd TS, the unit has 17 F-16 Fighting Falcons of various marks on strength which undertake complex test flights with new ordnance and control systems aimed at improving the overall effectiveness of the aircraft. This F-16A is devoid of all weapons, but mounts a 370 US gallon fuel tank under each wing. The visibility offered to the pilot through the large, tinted one piece canopy is clearly evident, and is one of the factors which endears this aircraft to its crews

Right Apart from the unusual paint scheme and the strange pods faired into the wing leading edge extensions, this F-16, plugged into a KC-135, looks like any other Fighting Falcon serving with the USAF. This machine is unique, however, being the only Advanced Fighter Technology Integration (AFTI) F-16 in existence

Below Converted from one of the Full Scale Development (FSD) F-16s built in 1975 by General Dynamics, the AFTI Falcon first flew in July 1982 and has spent the majority of its life at Edwards performing various tests. The agility of the F-16 is legendary, and this aircraft was the logical mount through which to test future manoeuvring concepts, the basic premise of the AFTI programme

Overleaf Besides the addition of two eight foot square canards beneath the intake, the AFTI F-16 has also had the fuselage spine beefed up to further enhance the agility of the aircraft. Despite its experimental configuration, the AFTI F-16 is still fully combat capable, hence the pair of AIM-9L Sidewinders mounted on the wing-tip pylons

Inset Gear tucked away, the back-seater in this specially modified F-16B peers out across the vast expanses of the Edwards locale as his pilot steadily climbs to operational height. Emblazoned with Air Defense Fighter (ADF) titles and wearing subdued squadron codes, this F-16B has been thoroughly tested as the prototype for 270 specially converted Alpha and Bravo model Fighting Falcons which are being issued to 11 Air National Guard fighter interceptor squadrons to replace F-4s and F-106s. The ADF F-16s have improved cruise missile combatability, state-of-the-art satellite navigation aids and have been made compatible with the AIM-7 Sparrow and AIM-120 AMRAAM missiles

Main picture Many missile firings have been performed by the 6512nd TS's F-16s in conjunction with the ADF programme. Mounted on the inner wing pylon, a specially marked AIM-7F Sparrow is fired by the pilot. The Air National Guard has already received some of the specially updated F-16s, with all deliveries from General Dynamics expected to be completed by Fiscal Year 1992

Another project currently underway involving the F-16 at Edwards is the Auto Terrain-Following (ATF) LANTIRN compatibility programme which has seen the Fighting Falcon equipped with the Strike Eagle avionics pods. The weapons load on this F-16A consists of a wing-tip mounted AIM-9P Sidewinder and an AGM-65 Maverick air-to-surface missile affixed to the outer pylon

Right Although the wing area on the F-16 is not over large, a fair swag of ordnance can nevertheless be hung underneath the aircraft. Besides the pair of Sidewinder AAMs, four experimental anti-tank bomblet pallets are also mounted on a twin hard-point pylon.

Below right Close up view of the two Sidewinder missiles, the one under the wing equipped with a seeker head, whilst the wing-tip weapon is devoid of the vital sensor

Below To obtain accurate data on the aircraft's speed, altitude and general flight parameters during testing, a special ultra-sensitive probe is fitted to the Fighting Falcon

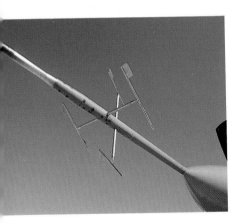

With the A-16 'Strike' Falcon proposal assuming greater priority with the USAF, several programmes concerning the compatibility of various attack orientated avionics hardware with the F-16 have been shown to be very worthwhile indeed. This F-16D is carrying the extremely effective LANTIRN targeting pod beneath the intake, an essential part of any low-level strike avionics suite for the proposed 'Strike' Falcon. The extensively instrumented test probe seen in the last photograph is also mounted to this aircraft

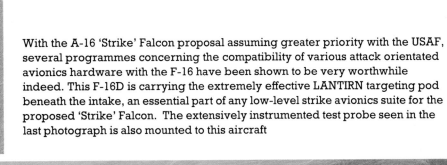

Left The versatility of the F-16 is perfectly illustrated in this photo. The wing-tip mounted AIM-9Ps combine with the internally fitted General Electric M61A-1 20 mm Vulcan cannon to give the Fighting Falcon formidable bite in the air-to-air scenario. The six AGM-65 Maverick missiles fitted snugly beneath each wing are deadly weapons against ground targets, whilst the two 370 US gallon tanks extend the already impressive range of the Fighting Falcon appreciably. The centreline pylon has an electronic countermeasures (ECM) pod attached to it to assist the aircraft's own inbuilt ECM avionics in combatting enemy radar

Above Today's test pilot explains the intricacies of his state-of-the-art office to a couple of potential future jet jocks

The ultimate bombers?

An awesome sight at any time, this Rockwell B-1B looks even more ominous in the low light of the early morning sun. Virtually all flight testing of the B-1 was carried out jointly by the manufacturer and the Air Force at Edwards over a period of ten years. This B-1 is plugged into the ground power and air-conditioning units which are vital to the successful pre-flighting of the bomber by both the ground and flight crews. Devoid of the white refuelling reference marks on the nose, this B-1B is an early production aircraft

The B-1 is a deceptively big aircraft, just how big being graphically emphasized in this head on view. The substantial intakes for the four General Electric F101-GE-102 augmented turbofan engines clutter an otherwise smooth underfuselage area, the positioning of the paired engine nacelles contrasting markedly with the stealthy approach taken by Northrop with the B-2. The sturdiness of the undercarriage may also be appreciated from this low-down view

The swing wing of the B-1 is one of its most distinct, and impressive, features. It allows the crew to operate the bomber from short runways, the unswept wing having considerable bite into the air, whilst giving the aircraft an impressive low-level penetration speed when in the fully swept position. Both wings are connected to the fuselage by the fixed wing carry-through box, a massive structure which, like the wings, doubles as an integral fuel tank. The box itself is made of diffusion-bonded 6AL-4V titanium, the same material that is used for the wing pivot mechanism

Left The beautifully smooth curves of the B-1B's upper fuselage are clearly evident as the pilot carefully nudges his way towards the refuelling boom

Right The sonic shock waves build up around the four powerful General Electric F-101s as the pilot hauls the big bomber around in an eye-wateringly tight high speed turn at low level over the Edwards range. The small swept-back movable vanes on the nose of the B-1 form part of the structural mode control system (SMCS) which helps improve the ride quality of the aircraft at low level. The vanes correct the pitching of the nose and are constructed of graphite epoxy bonded to aluminium honeycomb, with titanium employed for the leading and trailing edges

Overleaf Flying at a height of about 500 feet, a B-1B assigned to the test squadron at Edwards drops an inert B83 nuclear device from its forward weapons bay. Developed over the past nine years, the B83 is a 2400 lb weapon which is classed as a megaton device. It entered operational service in 1984 and is replacing the older B28 and B43 weapons developed in the 1950s. As can be seen here, the B83 is parachute-retarded and can be delivered at any altitude from 150 to 50,000 feet. The bomb carrying capacity of the B-1 is truly impressive, especially when compared to its predecessor, the

B-52 Stratofortress. The venerable Boeing bomber can carry four gravity bombs in its weapons bay whereas the B-1 can haul as many as 24, depending on the weight and size of the device in question. Flying alongside the B-1 acting as chase aircraft is an F-111A from the 6512nd TS

Inset, overleaf Rockwell technicians and USAF groundcrew wait patiently as the B-1 is refuelled and the systems checks completed. The large tail radome and smaller fin trailing edge cone are packed with sophisticated defensive avionics. Forming part of the AN/ALQ-161 system, a total of 107 individual units

give the aircraft 360 degree threat coverage. The complete system is controlled by several digital computers which give a near-instantaneous response to threatening radar by either jamming the frequency, or ejecting chaff and/or flares to clutter the aircraft's signal. The upper cone contains a tail warning radar, while the radome is packed with defensive avionics system transmitting antennae

Inset left preceding page On approach to one of several runways at Edwards, the pilot has swept the wings fully forward and deployed the trailing edge lift-augmenting devices in preparation for landing. The capacious forward bay is clearly marked by the white-outlined bay doors

Inset right preceding page
Surrounded by assorted pieces of ground clutter and plugged into various power units, a production B-1B sits quietly on the Edwards ramp. The Air Force has received all their B-1s from Rockwell, a total of 100 being delivered, although three have subsequently been lost in accidents. Four Strategic Air Command Bomb Wings are equipped with the B-1B; the 28th at Ellesworth, the 96th at Dyess, the 19th at Grand Forks and the 384th at McConnell

Preceding pages The four-man crew of the B-1B stands proudly in front of their mount. Besides the pilot and co-pilot, the B-1 is crewed by a pair of specialist systems operators; the Offensive Systems Operator (OSO), and the Defensive System Operator (DSO), both of whom are vital for the successful completion of the aircraft's primary mission. The crew boarding ladder is in the extended position on this B-1B

Right One of the travelling band of technicians who accompany the B-1B to Edwards from the Rockwell plant at Palmdale, California

Above Although the overall appearance of the B-1 fleet is rather drab, some individual aircraft, like this example from the 28th Bombardment Wing at Ellesworth, South Dakota, carry highly stylized artwork on their forward fuselage, albeit in low-vis colours! The weathering around the windscreen is quite severe for a relatively new aircraft like this B-1

History in the making. The ultimate in stealth technology, and the ultimate in
price, the bat-like Northrop B-2 finally parted company with terra firma, after an
abortive attempt a week earlier, on July 18 1989 at Edwards. Incorporating state
of the art materials in its structure, and having taken thousands of hours to
design, the B-2 does not come cheap, a total procurement of 132 aircraft for the
Air Force costing the tax payer a cool $500 million. The aircraft is powered by
four General Electric F118 engines, this powerplant being an unaugmented
turbofan based closely on the F110-GE-100 which powers the F-16C and the new
F-15E. These engines, buried stealthily into the inner wing areas either side of
the bulge which could be loosely termed the fuselage, reputedly give the B-2 an
impressive range of roughly 8000 miles, although this figure has not yet been
confirmed by Northrop or the USAF

Moments after take-off the Northrop test pilot climbs away from Edwards in his
unique mount. The jagged wing planform can be clearly seen in this view, as
can the sturdy, multi-wheeled undercarriage gear, the pilot leaving the aircraft
in this 'dirty' configuration for the entire flight. Six aircraft are to be assigned to
the flight testing programme, five of these eventually reverting to operational
use. The B-2 is designed to relieve the B-1B of the manned penetrator tasking
currently assigned to it by SAC. The B-1 will then become the stand-off missile
carrier, allowing the veteran B-52 fleet to be finally retired. The B-2 is scheduled
to enter squadron service in the mid-1990s, a time span which is looking
increasingly doubtful as the overall programme falls further and further behind
schedule

Mighty helpers

Below Looking as pristine as it did 32 years ago when it was rolled out of Boeing's Renton plant, NKC-135A 55-3122 taxies past the tower bathed in the afternoon sun. The fifth KC-135A manufactured, this aircraft has spent much of its life at Edwards, being the first Stratotanker handed over to the USAF for them to test. Belonging to the Aeronautical Systems Division, who are part of Air Force Systems Command, the NKC-135's parent unit is based at Wright-Patterson, Ohio, but along with a sister-ship, it spends most of its time flying above the parched expanses of California

Two of the oldest types in service with the USAF combine to test the effects of icing around the windscreen on B-52s. Using its refuelling boom, the crew of an Aeronautical Systems Division (ASD) NKC-135A spray water over a closely following B-52H, the liquid particles soon turning into ice at the height these aircraft are flying. The B-52 has a weapons pylon fitted beneath the port wing, a device which can carry either conventional bombs or cruise missiles

Above Of a much younger vintage, but far less colourful, McDonnell Douglas KC-10A Extender of the 9th Air Refueling Squadron (ARS) illustrates the current technology in air-to-air refuelling USAF style. The Extender is the military derivative of the DC-10-30CF convertible passenger/freighter, 59 of which survive in service out of a total of 60 delivered, one having been destroyed in a ground fire at Barksdale in September 1987. Besides the 9th ARS, which is based at March, the 32nd ARS at Barksdale and the 911th ARS at Seymour-Johnson also utilize the KC-10. The Extender can transfer an impressive 238 236 lbs of fuel to customers, as well as being able to accommodate 27 USAF Type 463L pallets, with a corresponding reduction in the fuel load

One of the original batch of 29 airframes constructed, NKC-135A 55-3128 is just a touch younger than its ASD companion. The nose of this aircraft has been modified at some time during its long career to carry a more sophisticated radar, and a mysterious bulge has also appeared beneath the fuselage just behind the boom operators prone position. As with the previous NKC-135, this Stratotanker is part of the 4950th Test Wing at Wright-Patterson. Hooked up is a 6512nd TS RF-4C proving that although this NKC-135A has fancy letters within its designation, a flashy ASD paint job and the odd lump and bump, it is still a Stratotanker!

Limited edition Hercules

A design that has been around for well over 30 years, the ubiquitous C-130 Hercules is currently being put through its paces at Edwards once again, but this time in the modified form of the MC-130H. Designated a *Combat Talon II* aircraft, the basic C-130H transport, as produced by Lockheed at their Georgia plant, is flown to Lockheed Air Services in California where various equipment is installed to allow the Hercules to perform day and night infiltration, psychological operations, aerial reconnaissance and the resupply of ground forces. Wearing Edwards codes on the fin, a suitably modified *Combat Talon II* MC-130H climbs away from the runway as the flight crew begin another operational evaluation sortie

Showing off its effective multi-coloured Europe One camouflage scheme against a scrub and sand backdrop, an MC-130H from the 6512nd TS cruises beneath the author. Being destined for the clandestine world of the US Special Operations Force (SOF), the *Combat Talon II* MC-130s have a suitably impressive avionics suite. Based on the package developed for the now-abandoned HH-60D Night Hawk helicopter, it includes an Emerson AN/APQ-170 digital radar with terrain-following/terrain-avoidance modes, ground map and beacon and weather modes; a Texas AAQ-15 Infra-red detector; dual inertial navigation equipment and radar altimeters; a comprehensive electronic countermeasures suite, plus provision for a global positioning satellite receiver. The MC-130 is in-flight refuelling capable, has a special cargo handling system installed, plus a high-speed low-level aerial delivery facility, with strakes and fairings around the rear ramp area which permit cargo drops to be made at speeds greater that 150 knots. A total of 24 MC-130Hs have been ordered by the SOF, deliveries of which commenced last year. The SOF already has a fleet of 14 MC-130Es equipped to *Combat Talon I* standard which were delivered in the mid 1970 s

Above The essential part of the Fulton System is the helium balloon, here being inflated by Edwards technicians before a test recovery. The system was developed jointly by the US Army and Air Force in the early 1960s under the title of Project 'Sky Hook'. Since its introduction in 1964 over 200 live extractions have been performed with only one fatal lift-line failure

One of the initial *Combat Talon I* MC-130Es sits on the ramp with its Fulton Recovery System aluminium forks deployed. This system, which has been omitted from the latest SOF aircraft, allows in-flight recovery of personnel from the ground. The precarious system utilizes a helium balloon attached to a strong cable, to the bottom of which the 'snatchee' is in turn harnessed. The Hercules approaches the cable at between 140 and 160 mph, locks the line between the forks and reels in the petrified occupant through the open rear cargo ramp. The lines attached to the nose of the aircraft prevent the cable from fouling the props should the forks fail to trap it. The modified nose of the MC-130E contains Terrain Following Radar which allows the aircraft to operate in all weathers down to a height of 250 feet. The Echo model MC-130 is operated exclusively by the 8th Special Operations Squadron, 1st Special Operations Wing, based at Hurlburt Field, Eglin Air Force Base, Florida

Right The Hercules is a big aircraft, but then the maintenance hangars at Edwards are also large. Beneath the sturdy tail section the groundcrew perform the early morning ritual of the FOD (foreign object debris) walkdown

Above A virtually brand new MC-130H taxies out past the tower before leaving Edwards. This particular Hercules is a bit of a mystery machine, having the in-flight refuelling receptacle fitted above the cockpit of the aircraft, but otherwise devoid of the Emerson radar nose. Furthermore, an unusual set of twin Loran (Long-range navigation) 'towel rack' antennae have been fitted to the dorsal fuselage area of the Hercules

The Hercules featured in the last photo drops a hefty load of pallets over the test range, the impressive cargo-carrying capability of the C-130 being graphically demonstrated

'Right Stuff' at ground level

Aircraft can be seen operating in the powder blue skies over Edwards all the time, but this is the high-profile, visible side of the base's overall testing function. Behind closed doors hundreds of technicians spend their time pushing the boundaries of aviation technology to its limits. Surrounded by aggressively patterned echo proof walls, an AIM-7F Sparrow missile guidance head is boresighted by a technician within an anechoic chamber. The chamber has been specially constructed to reduce echo reflection to virtually zero. The chamber can be designed to operate best at various wavelengths, with sound, ultrasound, microwaves and ultrasonic energy available, depending on the requirements of the system under test

The high-tech world of modern
aircraft simulators is beautifully
illustrated by this glowing F-16
avionics system installed at Edwards.
Flying in formation with a simulated
Fighting Falcon over the main runway
at the base, the pilot 'driving' the
computer prepares to pitch out for
landing

With Edwards being spread over such a vast expanse, and several test flights typically occurring at any given time, the range control centre has a vital role to play in the day to day running of the base. Surrounded by various displays and close-circuit television monitors, two civilian controllers ensure that the aircraft out on the range stay well away from each other

Left How to get away with flying a fast jet in shirt sleeves! A highly experienced ex-Sabre pilot flies a drone QF-86 over Edwards from the comfort of an air-conditioned operations building. The drone Sabre has had a long and distinguished career at the base, being used to measure the accuracy of new and improved guided missiles. The Sabres fly over a fully instrumented range and the miss distance of the weapon is measured with extreme accuracy. Often the QF-86 is equipped with cameras to film the missiles' trajectory.

Right Considering the futuristic nature of the flight testing carried out at Edwards you wouldn't expect the vital support facilities, like the all-important control tower, to be any less modern. A stylish structure to say the least, the tower is packed with sophisticated air traffic control gear, and provides a completely unobstructed view of the base ramp, and associated runways, for its occupants

Above Armed with a powerful pair of binoculars, a controller watches the progress of an incoming flight at dusk intently

Above right Looking remarkably like an old anti-aircraft position that once festooned the sides of aircraft carriers and battleships in the Pacific theatre of World War 2, a civilian operator shows off her 'driving position' on one of the many range telescopic tracking cameras which dot the base. These units provide real time coverage of test for ground-based technicians, both civilian and military, back at the Edwards facility. The high resolution cameras are protected when not in use by a weatherproof dome

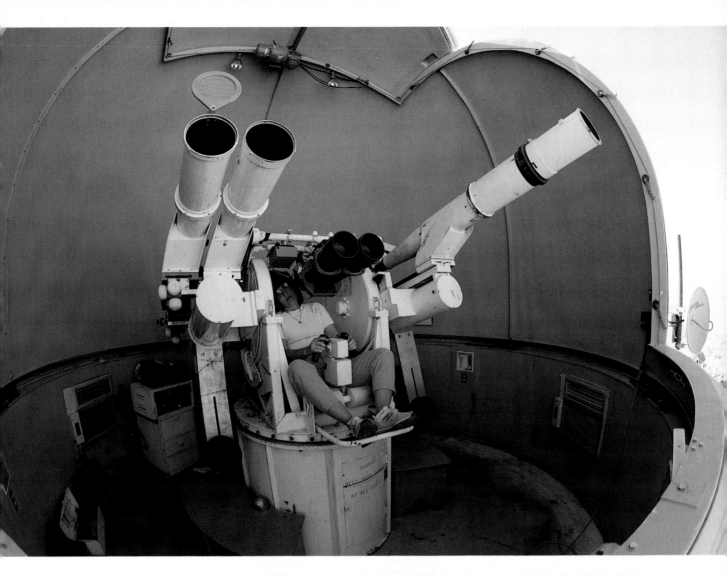

Right Combat bite of a different kind! Maybe a touch smaller than an Eagle or a Fighting Falcon, but no less deadly, a security police squadron German Shepherd is let loose by his sergeant to tackle an uninvited guest on the Edwards ramp

If diversification is what you want, then diversification is what yoúre going to get! A mouth-watering line up of exotic types catch the last rays of sunlight on the crowded ramp. It's not too often you get to see a Piper Cub alongside A-7s, F-4s and T-38s

A visor down, Ray-Bans on situation
for the crews of the KC-135, the two
F-16Bs and the drivers of the support
trucks as they all taxi out as one onto
the runway

Left The remarkably flat surrounds of Edwards dominate the test squadron T-38 and F-4E parked in the foreground

Above It is an odds on bet that none of these aircraft are less than 15 years old! The accumulated flying hours of this little lot would be a rather large figure. The numerous ground support trolleys spread across the ramp add a rather hectic air to the Edwards pan

Testing time

Main picture An example of getting it right the first time, the remarkable Northrop T-38 Talon provides the vital link between new postings to the 6512nd Test Squadron and actually flying the unit's high performance types. With the instructor already seated, the 'pupil' climbs aboard while the crew chief, hands on hips, waits to help him with his plethora of retaining straps. The word pupil is a term used loosely, all potential test pilots previously having flown fast jets to an exceptional standard for many years

Inset Manufactured at Northrop's Palmdale plant as part of block number 85 over 19 years ago, Talon 70-1558 heads up a tight row of fellow test pilots school T-38s

Above left Wearing his fighter jock Ray-Bans and carrying his flight bag and helmet, Colonel Vern Saxon, squadron CO, strides out with a fellow Talon pilot to commence a sortie over Edwards

Below left Long before the flight is commenced the tireless groundcrew are busily swarming all over the aircraft completing the final tasks to allow the pilot to depart on time. One of those tasks is the cleaning, both inside and out, of the capacious cockpit and canopy, the final spit and polish of the perspex hood being vigorously performed here by a suitably fatigued plane captain

Above right Wearing the latest in Air Force bone domes, both the pupil and the instructor perform their respective pre-flight checks before taxiing out from the ramp. Interestingly, only the pilot has rear vision strip-mirrors fixed to the frame of his canopy

Below right Everything is functioning as Northrop intended and the crew ladder lays on its side safely away from the aircraft. All that remains is for the prone groundcrewman to pull the chocks away from the main undercarriage wheels

Inset, overleaf Also on strength with the 6512nd, but in far smaller numbers than the T-38A, is the NOA-37B Dragonfly. Basically a beefed up T-37 Tweet trainer, the Dragonfly performs all manner of weapons tests, specifically for attack aircraft at the opposite end of the performance spectrum from the F-15E and B-1B. Carrying a pair of large external tanks and two 500 lb bombs under its wings, this NOA-37B has had its nose mounted refuelling probe replaced by a pitot tube. Having received the visual 'hands up' for a successful engine start, the crew will soon retract the large one piece canopy and enter the Edwards circuit

Overleaf, main picture Not possessing the most aerodynamically efficient fuselage and wing in the first place, this NOA-37B is really making life difficult for itself carrying both tip and wing tanks, plus a pair of Rockeye cluster bombs. The full range of communications and forward air control avionics are housed in the various black lumps and blisters which festoon the central fuselage. This Dragonfly differs from the previous example as it still retains the factory fitted nose refuelling probe

Below right Another machine that is not noted for its overwhelming numerical presence at Edwards is the diminutive Beech T-34C Turbo Mentor. Retaining the colours of its parent service, the US Navy, this particular Turbo Mentor is one of several operated by the Army as part of its test and development unit based at Edwards. Concerned mainly with helicopter trials work, the pilots nevertheless retain their fixed wing rating by flying regularly in the T-34C. In the 1950s and 60s the Army used similarly painted ex-Navy T-28 Trojans to fulfil a similar role

Performance helicopters

Frighteningly awesome are words that immediately spring to mind when viewing the McDonnell Douglas (formerly Hughes) AH-64A Apache from virtually any angle. Developed essentially to fulfil a programme formulated in 1964, the Apache has been in service now for over four years, giving the US Army a virtually trouble free run in that time. The helicopter first operated from Edwards in June 1976 when, as the Hughes YAH-64, it successfully saw off its major rival, the Bell YAH-63, in the Army's rigorous competitive evaluation trials. The substantial size of the stub wings can be appreciated in this view of the helicopter hovering amongst the hills out on the range

Insets The multiplicity of blade aerials, sensors, electronic warfare devices and weaponry are silhouetted against the pastel colours of the evening sky. The relatively small diameter of the rotor blades is one of the unique features of the Apache

Main picture Armed with the deadly Rockwell Hellfire AGM-114A anti-tank missile and the 19 shot FFAR (folding-fin aircraft rocket) tube, plus the potent Hughes M230A-1 Chain Gun specially developed for this helicopter, a drab Apache of the Army test flight banks tightly towards the author, the pilot occupying the back seat staring down the camera lens

Above The Army's workhorse of the eighties, the Sikorsky UH-60 Black Hawk also maintains a presence at Edwards, development and support work being its major functions at the base. Offering perfect camouflage in a jungle combat situation, the drab Army green retains the heat rather uncomfortably well in the high California desert, much to the chagrin of the sweaty crews

Right The violent dusk sky seems to mirror the potential havoc that the Apache can create for the unsuspecting enemy tank crew. The helicopter is continually being evaluated by both the Army and McDonnell Douglas at Edwards in an effort to improve its already impressive performance, and increase its weapons compatibility. Tests were recently completed here, and at Marine Corps Air Station Yuma, concerning the carriage of the AIM-9 Sidewinder, a missile the helicopter is now officially allowed to carry

Even the humble Huey, in this case a twin UH-1N, is flown by the 6512nd at Edwards, both as a test vehicle and as a search and rescue helicopter. The fancy, yet functional, scheme on this twin Huey is a variation on the squadron's white and red colours which predominate on most of the unit's aircraft

Edwards oddities

Main picture Possibly the most famous 'transient' at Edwards is the Space Shuttle, the majority of the vehicle's recoveries from orbit taking place on the seemingly endless dry lake bed runways which criss-cross the base. Showing signs of the intense heat build up around the nose, the recently arrived *Discovery* is towed back to the huge NASA hangars for a thorough post-mission check

Inset A Shuttle with a difference! The motive power of a large USAF GMC prime-mover is used to haul the Shuttle crash training mock-up fuselage out of its hangar. This full size aid is used by the base's emergency services

Main picture A sight to gladden the heart of any sixties heavy metal freak. Painted up resplendently in full NASA colours, a brace of veteran F-104 Starfighters formate tightly above the desolate scrubland of California. The F-104G has an unusual fillet shaped device fitted beneath its fuselage. The cannon blister for the internally mounted M61 gun has been faired over as the weapon itself would have been removed many years ago

Inset Taxiing past the tower with both hinged canopies open to aid crew ventilation, this elegant TF-104G is the second civilian registered two-seater on strength with the Ames-Dryden Flight Research Facility at Edwards. These aircraft operate in support of the Space Shuttle research programme and are maintained in immaculate condition

Left A monument to former glory days at Edwards, a polished NF-104A arches towards the wild blue yonder. This airframe is one of three Alpha models converted by Lockheed and flown in a series of successful zoom to altitude flights. A small LR-121/AR-2 rocket engine was installed in the base of the fin and pushed the Starfighter to a height of 103,000 feet. Special shock cones were fitted to the engine intakes to accommodate higher mach speeds and a metal nose cone, housing reaction control system flight aids to combat excessive pitch and yaw, was also added. One of these aircraft was lost spectacularly during a record breaking flight by the legendary Chuck Yeager. The baking sun has taken its toll on this unique airframe, but the Starfighter is regularly polished and painted, a fitting tribute to the pilots who lost their lives at Edwards

A mixture of the operational and the experimental entertains the crowds sweltering out on the line at the 1988 Edwards Open House. The radically different Grumman X-29 has completed over 110 flights since arriving at Edwards several years ago. An advanced technology demonstrator (ATD), the aircraft has swept-forward wings to explore various flight parameters

Left The X-29 is currently in the midst of an extensive new test phase exploring very high angle-of-attack (AOA) flights. A total of $7.5 million has been spent by Grumman to modify it for these tests and it has been cleared to fly at up to 70 degrees. A second X-29 is also being phased into the programme

Right From the radical to the conventional. Several virtually standard Vought A-7D Corsair IIs are regularly used by the 6512nd to test new types of ordnance, and delivery patterns associated with these weapons. The A-7 also makes an exemplary chase aircraft for new types undertaking low-level testing

Below right Having successfully lowered an inert Mk 83 iron bomb from one loading trolley onto another, the armourer unshackles the weapon. This particular A-7 is fitted with a highly sensitive calibration probe to measure the pitch and yaw of the aircraft during the flight

Another programme currently underway at Edwards centres around the mission adaptive wing manufactured by Boeing and mounted on an Aeronautical Systems Division F-111. Part of the grandly titled Advanced Fighter Technology Integration (AFTI) series of tests, the specially modified F-111 has raked up an impressive total of flying hours with the new wing. The tests have seen four automated flight control modes for the wing evaluated including manoeuvre camber control, cruise camber control, manoeuvre load control and manoeuvre alleviation/gust enhancement. These modes are aimed at determining the best aerodynamic efficiency and minimum drag levels of the wing, as well as increasing its capability to pull G and giving the F-111 an overall lift in its agility. The ride for the crew, and their ability to deliver the weapons on target, is also improved